WRITERS REPUBLIC

The Anointed One

Poetry, Prose & Lessons Vol.1

JADAZESHA SHARP

WRITERS REPUBLIC L.L.C.
515 Summit Ave. Unit R1
Union City, NJ 07087, USA

Website: *www.writersrepublic.com*
Hotline: *1-877-656-6838*
Email: *info@writersrepublic.com*

Ordering Information:
Quantity sales. Special discounts are available on quantity purchases by corporations, associations, and others. For details, contact the publisher at the address above.

Library of Congress Control Number: 2021930637
ISBN-13:   978-1-63728-172-7   [Paperback Edition]
                  978-1-63728-173-4   [Digital Edition]

Rev. date: 01/08/2021

I am grateful that God has guided me through every step and I am also grateful that my family has come along the way. To my grandmother who listens to every new and crazy idea with an open heart.

Last but not least, I am thankful for the people that have entered my life and have already taught me so much.

Contents

PREFACE

There have been three words that I can tell you have deeply impacted my life. Those words are darkness, rising and walking. I have had times in my life where everything felt really dark and then I have had times where things felt much better. Truthfully, we go through periods of a mixture of good and bad times.

I felt out of tune with myself as I went through these different times in my life. So, the process of writing this book has been one of emotional hardship and triumph. Some days it was a challenge to go through the emotions of my past while looking toward the joys of the future. There were many days where all of my emotions overwhelmed me. I struggled to release them. But the process of writing this book has guided me to myself. It has led me to pieces of me that I wasn't quite sure of but happy to see. So, I say this book has pieces of me through my poetry writing and lessons from God.

I wouldn't desire to really tell you about something that I have not experienced. I want to share my real true experiences. I've had to sit back and evaluate the areas of my life that seemed too much to handle. I've had to make decisions that were meant to grow me and move me to better places. I want to take you on my journey through my story. I want to show you what it meant for me to move from a place of darkness to a place of light.

DARKNESS

NO SUNRAYS OVER HERE

Where is the light

I can't seem to find it

Where is the heat

It's freezing down here

With no hope and no joy

It's winter down here.

FEAR

Just like that

I never sat

In my tears

With my fears

They were suppressed away

Not to interrupt my day

But now I have no choice

But to look at these fears (that were unvoiced).

SEEN AND HEARD

I see you

    And I hear you.

I don't understand myself

    But I'm trying to understand you.

I'm trying to connect to you

    Without first connecting with me.

So, I keep wondering why

    These emotional connections

        Are not working out.

FAILURE

A shame

But I really have no one to blame

My ego, my pride

It kept me all tied

I thought I had it all together

But the storms I couldn't weather

They threw me under the bus

With nothing left to discuss

See my ego, my pride

I used as my guide

Told me not to ask for help

Because that's what failures yelp

So, I stayed to the side

With teary eyes that dried

And my pride, that lied.

WHIRLWIND

How do I escape

an endless amount of emotions?

Fear, anxiety, sadness,

anger, hurt all

wrapping around my happiness,

my joy

and

my

peace.

WHERE ARE THEY

I'm looking for a superhero

Don't they save lives or so?

I'm looking for a superhero

I need help, you know

TUGGING ON LIFE

I'm tugging for something

But I have it all wrong

I'm tugging for something

That's not meant for me

I'm going in the wrong direction

But I didn't know

I thought I was doing

What was meant for me

I thought I was living

My hopes and dreams

With desperate pleas

And on my knees.

GOOD ENOUGH

When will I ever be good enough?

I give and give, yet this world takes.

When will I ever reach the top? I look

on the sidelines cheering everyone

else on and I don't mind it. But my heart

and my mind won't let me rest there.

They ask about our God-given potential.

What about the things we can do?

What about the lives we can change?

What about our hopes and our dreams?

How much longer will we have to wait?

And I don't have an answer because

I'm still questioning if I'll have what it takes.

JUST EXISTING

I'm drinking away the pain

I'm drinking away the weekend

The bottle subdues the pain

But what about when it comes back?

How will I be able to answer the question,

What am I really living for?

DADS

Daddy's little girl

That's just a name

Daddy's little girl

I've never obtained

Daddy's little girl

My time was cut short

Daddy's little girl

Your advice

Your support

UNCERTAINTY

So, I'm looking out my window

and I see a city on fire. These

flames that are consuming it are

bright as the sun. I want to reach

my hand out just to feel the warmth.

I'm looking for a fire down deep

in my soul. I want to experience

something that gives me meaning

and hope. But I wonder if I'm entering

dangerous territory. You see, the problem

with stepping out there is that I have this

fear. I'm really trying to stay away from

getting burned.

HOPELESSNESS (?)

Who do I go to

When I need some help

Who do I go to

Where should I look

I need a kind savior

No cape is needed

A healing hand

To stress out these demons

I just want to be saved

In more ways than one

I have nothing left

It's pretty obvious to see

That if I don't get help

There'll be no more me.

LABELS

Do you choose when the sun rises

and when it sets? Do you choose

when the moon comes out? You try

to determine me with your labels,

but do you really know me? What

does it take for you to really get to know me?

RISING

UPROOTING

You can let it be pulled

You can let the leaves wilt

It's no longer growing you

It's no longer serving you

We need some new seeds

It's time for new planting.

MY HEALING TAKES TIME

My healing takes time.

My joy will be restored.

My hope will be restored.

My love will be restored.

My peace will be restored.

In time, I will be restored

to who I was always meant

to be.

WHAT ABOUT DROWNING?

As I was pulled into the water,

I thought I was going to drown.

There's something about not

being able to touch the ground.

I mean, I was so used to feeling

in over my head. I thought maybe

this is where I was being led.

I had it all wrong. This time

was going to be different. I was

going to float. I was going

to make it back to the shore.

SISTERHOOD

Some of

our sisters are connected

by flesh and blood

Some of our sisters

are connected

uniquely because of

your love

MOVE IN FREEDOM

I am set free

I am not my pain.

Anxiety you can't

have me

Fear you can't

have me.

GIANTS AND WARRIORS

In the midst of these battles,

I'm wondering if I really have

what it takes. Can I do this?

Can I face these giants standing

over me? These giants look ten

feet tall. They look like they

wouldn't even fall. Am I David?

NO BLOCKAGE NEEDED

Those dark and cloudy days used to fill me.

Yes, those dark and cloudy days of anxiety used

to fill me. Yes, those dark and cloudy days

of pain used to fill me. Yes, those dark and

cloudy days of unforgiveness used to fill me.

Yes, those dark and cloudy days of offense

used to fill me. Yes, those dark and cloudy

days of disappointment used to fill me. But

light is starting to come through

the clouds. I can see it clearly.

No, I'm no longer allowing my mind to be covered.

No, I'm no longer allowing my heart to be covered.

I'm starting to shine.

A FRESH START

I'm ready for a new day

I want a new start

This is my new beginning

This is a new hope

This is a new joy

This is a new love

This is a new peace.

WHAT WAS ONCE SPOKEN

Those words that

were once spoken,

are no longer needed.

I no longer need to

please people and

give away my truth.

I no longer need to

abandon all that

I am. So, I'm letting

go of all the old

arguments and

misunderstandings.

I'M RISING

Life tried to take me out

but I'm rising back up.

Struggles knocked me

around but I'm rising

back up. Fear tried to

suffocate me but I'm

rising back up.

I'm rising back up.

RELATIONSHIPS

Are you ready

for love? Are

you ready to let

someone build

with you? Are

you ready to

let someone

help you? Are

you ready to

let someone

grow with

you? Are you

ready to let

someone in?

HUMAN

You failed me

You disappointed me

You disregarded me

You made me feel

less than. You shut

me down. You

wounded me deeply

But you're imperfect

You're human.

Jadazesha Sharp

SIGNED, OVERCOMER

Fear and anxiety,

you have no place here

I will no longer be held

back by you.

WALKING

I'M WELCOMING YOU

Here you are.

You're finally here.

It seemed like it would've

taken forever to get to you.

But look at you, thriving

even now. I welcome you

to your purpose. I welcome

you to your life. I welcome

you to your hopes and

dreams. I welcome you

to you.

LONG STRIDES

I'm taking long

strides toward you.

I'm not rushing through

it, but I will jump, hop

and skip a little closer.

All because I love the

feelings and emotions

that I get from being

with my Father. All

because I love the

experiences that I

have with you. All

because I love the

hopes and dreams

that captivate my

soul when I'm with

you. So, I'm never

going back to the

way things used

to be.

EPHESIANS, JEREMIAH & ISAIAH

I am your workmanship.

You prepared good works

for me to move in, before

the foundations of the earth.

You know the end from the beginning.

You placed your purpose in me. Before

you formed me in my mother's womb,

you placed your purpose in me. You

called me to it. You set me apart. I was

made for this.

STAND

I actually have to

show up as me. I

have to stand in

my power. I have

to stand in who I am.

No more allowing people

to intimidate me. No more

feeling inferior to everyone

around me. No more

shrinking down. No more.

AN OPEN BOOK

Will I allow people

to read my pages?

Will they understand

the writing? Will they

follow along word for

word across the pages?

Will they get a mental

image?

BROTHERHOOD

Men need support too.

Underneath all that they are,

men need support too.

A brother, when it's difficult

to fathom their pain

A brother, who is there through

their losses and their gains.

BAREFOOT

I'm walking around barefoot

Not really sure where to set my foot

To fully and completely get back to you

To fully and completely show up as you

But maybe that's the point. Maybe my

feet are supposed to touch each level.

Maybe I'm supposed to move step by step.

THE PAST

It would no longer suit me to live

my life for you. I mean, it was some

kind of journey but now I'm

meant to live for me.

YOUR LOVE

Maybe I don't know much about love.

Maybe I don't understand what it feels

like unconditionally. Well, I thought I

didn't.

I see how you love me without

limits. I see how you move mountains

for me. I see how you don't let the fire

consume me.

BEST SELF

What do you see when you look at you?

I hope you see all of your potential. I hope you

see the man or woman you are meant to be.

I hope you rise up to the challenge. Let nothing

cause you to back down. Let no person cause you

to back down. You were made to be you.

LESSONS PART 1

LESSON 1 THE ENEMIES TO MY DESTINY

So, where do I start? I love my family members; like I really love them to the point that I would do anything for them. They are the ones I would usually go to for everything concerning my problems and my life. You know the people that you say are your rock; the people who you feel will always be there to pick you up. Yeah that was my family. But over this past year I began to see a shift in the way I saw them. I no longer saw them as the ones I could confide in or freely speak my hopes and dreams to.

A big problem got in the way of my relationship with my family. What was that problem you might ask or maybe not, but I'll tell you anyway. It was me. I was the big problem because I started this journey to see who I really was. I began to seek God for the personality traits and mannerisms that were truer to who I was compared to how I was so used to carrying myself. What I found began to surprise me but that's for later in the story.

I felt like one part of me was always this super smart and super sweet girl. I was always the "good" kid and the one making the best grades. Yeah, that's all fine and dandy when you are a kid but eventually, I became an adult who was still trying to hold on to those titles. I was an adult trying to make sure my family members approved of my decisions, my career choices and my life overall. I wanted to stay in their grace of knowing what's best based on what they experienced. But I wasn't seeing who I really was. I wasn't seeing my individual gifts and talents because I was holding on to what everyone else thought my gifts and talents would be.

It came time for me to stray from everyone else telling me about me. But it didn't happen without a fight, sadly. Funny story, I was so used to doing what everyone else wanted for my life that I literally had to be dragged to see that I wasn't living for myself. So, here is how it took place. If you know my first book you know that I mentioned I continued getting a degree in a career that I had no interest in. I was trying to please everyone else. Well, I went back and forth for four years forcing myself to be happy in something I just couldn't find joy in. Some would argue that I had many things to be happy about with this particular career choice and they could be right. But I whole-heartedly believe that you should not stay in a career choice that doesn't bring you the utmost fulfillment or some type of joy.

I tried to find an enjoyable area in the field that I spent four years disliking. That was half-heartedly my intentions at first, but it didn't work out. I cried, I complained, I sat around, and I wasted a lot of money preparing to do nothing with the degree that I received. I should have just chosen to go my own way but like I said I was so used to doing what everyone else thought was good for me.

I didn't see it at first, but I was learning just how much I was unwilling to speak up for myself and seek the life I wanted to live. I was so willing to put everyone else's desires, dreams and goals above my own that I couldn't see anything else. It's funny, trying to make sure everyone else dreams and goals or maybe deep down something that would make them feel good about themselves is being accomplished through you. But you end up on the flip side with no dreams and goals of your own rising to the top. That was just the rock bottom that God led me to over this past year.

How far was I willing to go for what everyone else wanted me to do? How far was I willing to lose myself in everyone else's life? I was willing to go pretty far, and I did go pretty far. I really didn't want to live the life I was living anymore. I was at a point where I surely didn't care if I lived or died. Some people would say that's taking it too far, but I say we all handle obstacles differently.

God met me at this very rock bottom. It took me a minute to realize it, but God had a whole plan for me once I hit that rock bottom. He had a whole plan for me before the rock bottom. But I wasn't really willing to give up everything that I was so used to, how I carried myself and how I lived for others until it just became too much. I began to see so much more for my life when I started surrendering living my life for others. I began to see a life that I never knew was possible.

Surrendering everything to God wasn't the easiest thing to do. I fought tooth and nail to hold on to what I thought about myself, to how my family members saw me/ how I showed up in the world. I mean of course I didn't want to stay living up under my family members wants and desires, but I really thought it made sense. It was literally all I knew. But God began to peel back layers of deeper issues.

I began to realize that not only was I used to doing what everyone else desired for me, it eventually became a cover up. I was afraid to venture out into the unknown where I would have to face the truth: **I didn't know who I was**. I would have to literally sit-down face to face with myself and learn who I was outside of performance. I would have to learn who I was outside of the traits I thought would make me or break me. I would have to learn my purpose in this world. All of these things made me more nervous when I realized I had to give up the strategies, the techniques and the coping skills that I held on to. I couldn't use the same tactics to learn about myself, to live my life and get different results.

I had to give up seeing my family as holding me back. Right? I had to decide to no longer care about their opinions whether we lived in the same house or not. I had to be intentional about what hopes and dreams I felt comfortable sharing with them. It's less about me not sharing my life with them and more about establishing boundaries with what I share. It's more about me allowing God to take me on this journey to learn more about myself regardless of what they think.

LESSON 2 EMOTIONAL CONNECTIONS: BRINGING BACK THE PAST

I didn't really understand how to have strong emotional connections with others. It's weird that I even had a romantic relationship with how closed off and guarded I was in some ways. Let me clarify, there were two different situations going on here.

I wasn't physically attracted to the person I was with. I also was so guarded that I couldn't accept affection properly. So, there was still some discomfort when my attraction began to grow. In the beginning of the relationship, I struggled to accept hugs, sitting close to one another or even when it came to compliments. I didn't feel comfortable giving compliments at all. I also felt really awkward when a compliment was given to me.

It was easier for me to show my affection from a distance. I could send cute messages and give thoughtful gifts. But I struggled when it came to speaking loving words out loud such as I love you and I care about you. I would say it mostly through text messages because it felt too awkward to say face to face. I don't want to make it seem like we just sat there and stared at each other for three years. But part of me knew that it was hard to connect with him on a deeper level because of my parents. I remember one time, my dad dropped me off at my ex-boyfriend's house. Clear as day a thought ran in my head as I looked toward the window that maybe I can't really let him in emotionally and to the full capacity as I should be able to because I don't even have a deeper relationship with my dad.

So, let's talk about my relationship with my parents. You know as kids we want our mother and father's attention. We might do silly things to get their attention, we cry, we whine, we scream, we shout, etc. We do certain things to let them know that we have needs. I was that little girl waiting for my parents to meet my needs and there were just some that they couldn't meet. A little back story on my parents: They were very young when they had me. My mom wanted space after I was born. My dad wanted marriage after I was born.

My parents split up and my great grandmother was given full custody of me. My parents were still in my life and that is where it became complicated. I couldn't understand why I could see my mom and see my dad but then not feel so close to them. There was a point in time where I thought my parents were the coolest. I wanted to follow them around the house and just do everything they were doing. But it felt like I was outside of their life, like I wasn't fully engaged in their life. I felt like I became the child who was left to the side while they chased after their life. I felt like I became the child that they saw on the weekends or doing free time but really left all the work of raising me to everyone else.

I had grandparents, aunts, and uncles to be there for me, but I still wanted my parents in on it. I wanted my mom and dad to really see me. I wanted them to see me and show up for me in the way everyone else was. The truth of the matter is I needed it.

I needed my parents along the way when I began to feel lost. The moment I began kindergarten, another person was entering my life who just didn't know how to meet my needs. My teacher was an aggressive person and I wasn't too fond of her. So, I learned to play two different roles to cope with it. I was shy, quiet and a very good student in school. At home, I was more talkative and playful. It seems like there is nothing wrong with these two roles but it's a problem when you stop expressing yourself. I was allowing myself to truly express myself at home. But in school and any location outside of home was where I kept up this other version of myself.

Some might say this is nothing serious and you should have been able to get past something so long ago. Honestly, it sounded a little silly to me until I realized what I was doing. I began to merge the two roles to the point where I didn't know how to fully be me. I was so comfortable showing a version of me that I formed to cope with life as a kid. But it wasn't serving me as an adult.

I could tell it's been a problem over this past year when my family members would make comments of me being the sweetest and the kindest. It was a shock to them when I would step out of that little bubble. It showed me that they were determining parts of who I am based on the persona that I showed for so long. I began to realize that I've been giving them an image of me that wasn't really me freely and to the full capacity. In fact, I was giving the whole world an image of me that wasn't freely and fully me to the full capacity.

When God began to bring other people in my life, I couldn't connect with them. Not only was I not being my full self, but I was also putting myself beneath people. I saw these people as better than me. I put them on a pedestal where I didn't think I could ever fit in with them. I didn't think I belonged with them. That was really how I was seeing most people in my life. I couldn't form any real true emotional connections with people if I saw myself as beneath all of them.

LESSON 3 WHO'S THIS LITTLE GIRL

As an adult I could still see the broken little girl and her issues. In fact, I had no problem mentioning that I felt like that broken little girl to a few people I trusted. I didn't realize how much truth it held. I didn't realize how much it meant in my life until I saw how little I was living my life. I wouldn't do certain things. I wouldn't apply for certain jobs and I wouldn't speak to certain people all because of the fear that I carried on the inside. I didn't self-sabotage friendships, but I wasn't building any because I couldn't fathom what I had that people would want. I couldn't see people really wanting to enjoy my company and being around me just for who I was.

So, I went all throughout high school and college not really building any deep or true friendships with people. I went all throughout high school and college afraid to speak boldly and confidently about my beliefs. I was afraid to be spontaneous, to try new things and to basically live life. I hadn't engaged in many experiences that people my age would have done. I was too afraid to venture out into the world and live for more than the safety and comfortability that I was so used to.

Who was this little girl living my life for me? Why was she walking around as an adult but couldn't handle the adult issues? For so long, I was allowing the little girl in me to show up in the world: a little girl who was surrounded by fear, social anxiety, perfectionism, abandonment and rejection. I couldn't even see who I could be past all the childhood traumas and insecurities. For so long, I felt lonely and isolated from others. I couldn't even understand what it felt like to have fulfilling relationships. This explains the relationship I put myself in. It was full of brokenness because two broken people who had no business coming together met. No matter how much effort I put into the relationship, my brokenness was still going to pop out. There was nothing I could do about it because I wasn't addressing that it all started with my mom and dad. Same wise for my dating partner, his brokenness was showing up in issues that he wasn't addressing.

It came to a point where I could no longer sit back and ignore the little girl in me. Honestly, God made me sit down to really see the scared and insecure little girl. I mean really see her for all that she was. She couldn't talk to people in deeper and emotional ways and she couldn't let people love her for all that she was. She couldn't see what value she had to add to the world around her. She couldn't see that she wasn't stupid, and she wasn't slow.

She couldn't see that the things she did took more time for her to comprehend and she wasn't stupid for needing more time to get it. She just processed some things at a slower pace and needed time to evaluate. I couldn't see that I was made to be a deep thinker with all the love of God in my heart. He made me with all my silliness and all my goofiness. He made me with all my cheerfulness and all my uniqueness.

So I found myself in adulthood with no friendships, but I craved one best friend. I wanted someone to hang out with, go out to eat with and do silly things together. I wanted someone to see me for who I really was and not turn away when I showed them the pieces of me that didn't look so pleasant. I wanted someone to really desire to get to know me and not hang out with me because they pitied me. But most of all I wanted someone to accept all of me and never try to change me or shape me to fit into what they desired of me.

Honestly, I thought the type of friendship I wanted had sailed. I mean at my age now; people are so focused on careers and some starting families. I just thought that desire of my heart had passed. But what I didn't realize until now is that there are people sometimes connected to your purpose. So, whatever things you think may have sailed and whatever relationships you felt you may have personally self-sabotaged may just come back around.

I wanted to stand boldly in my purpose and not back down because of difficulty. I wanted to live so passionately in my purpose that nothing could stop it. Yet, I was afraid to even step out there for it. I wanted to speak the truth for Christ but would let every insecurity and fear of me being the one to do that get in the way. What if I didn't understand this much about the bible? What if I didn't get the full context that I feel like I should have down pack? What if no one wants to listen to someone that looks like me and acts like me?

The truth is who I've always been has liked to joke and laugh even in the midst of seriousness. Joking and laughing takes the tension off of things for me. I feel more in my element when I can be playful and when I can crack jokes. This part of me was what the younger version of me didn't know to hang on to. This part of me was always meant to show up.

I wanted to live spontaneously and uniquely to how it felt in my heart. But I was afraid that I would be seen as weird or someone who always had her head in the clouds. People fascinated me to no extent with the way they carried themselves, the way they dressed and the way they communicated with others. I wanted to see the hope and the potential in people. I wanted to help them see their potential. But along the way I began to lose understanding of what I truly desired. I tried to take on their problems and fix them for them.

I remember when I was probably 18 or a little younger, my mom told me that I didn't see reality; like I was living in this fantasy land of life. I also remember one time my dad told me to stop posting motivational quotes on my Facebook page because it shows people that I have problems. They just didn't see the deeper meaning to it. I may not have had the best way of expressing what I felt was placed in me, but I knew there was something in my heart and soul.

There was something deep down in me that knew I was supposed to uplift others in some shape or form, I just didn't know in what way. There was something deep down that knew I was supposed to live a life that was different. The younger version of me knew this. I was always daydreaming and hoping for something more.

I always dreamed of me doing something that everyone would pay attention to. I always dreamed of having my own family even as little as 12 years old. I wanted my own family so much so that I loved babysitting my little cousin and watching newborn delivery shows at 12 years old.

I was passionate about a lot of things and found it hard to stick to one thing. I know now that I want to do many powerful things in this world. I don't want to be a one-track kind of girl. I don't want to settle in my life. God had to bring me back into remembrance of that little girl's hopes and dreams even as I'm writing this. Sometimes we can let the environments that cultivate us dampen us. Sometimes life bogs us down so much that we wonder what's the point of dreaming like that or believing like that.

But really one of the biggest lessons that I learned over the past year is that you can still grow and develop beautifully in a pile of mess. God told me "I can grow you in a place that couldn't grow you." He said, "I can grow you in a place that isn't growing." Those words stuck to me because he really cared so much about me to dig into things that I didn't know was hurting me and bring up things I didn't even remember I wanted. Words can't even explain the amount of love that I felt God had for me in those very moments to really bring back the hopes and dreams that I ached for as a little girl. I came to the realization that I didn't have to stay stuck in the traumas of my past, but I just needed to come into agreement with the healing and growth that would need to take place.

LESSONS PART 2

LESSON 4 HELLO, ME

Who is it that God says I am? What does God know about me that I don't know about me? Am I willing to follow what God says about me regardless of what I look like to everyone else? God began to tell me things about myself that I didn't even think fully aligned with how people saw me. It didn't even align with how I saw me. This was the reintroduction to the new and improved me.

I loved music as a kid but as I grew up you would never catch me getting on the dance floor. I loved listening to rhythms and drum beats to songs by the time I was in high school. I would tap on anything I could get my hands on just because I thought it was fun. I wanted to see how many different beats I could come up with which led to my desire to play percussion instruments in high school. Rewind back to elementary school, I was recreating pictures that my art teacher gave to the class. My teacher would sit next to me and watch me draw the picture that she placed near me. I loved looking at images and recreating them piece by piece, but I wasn't the best at adding my own little twist to the pictures.

Rewind back a little more, I was the kid jumping around the house and laughing at whatever I thought was funny. I would jump off a stack of pillows only to land on my head. I would reflect constantly on my day at school and didn't mind sharing every detail of it. My great grandmother described me in the nicest way she could, as someone who would never stop talking. So, when God began to reintroduce me to who I really was, I didn't know how much of it really did pertain to pieces of my childhood.

Most of the pieces of me I wasn't fully showing to the world were hidden away with my childhood. I realized my great grandmother was the one that fully and completely saw all sides of me before life stepped in the way. She saw the raw parts of me, the unpleasant parts of me and the most loving parts of me. It was at this realization that God told me to go back to that little girl version of me. He gave me a mental picture of the address, the neighborhood and the memories that I needed for that age. I was my truest self in those very moments.

We look at kids and see how carefree they are. But what I really didn't take notice of is that they have the freedom to be their truest selves. They are able to truly and freely express themselves. How many times do we hold back expressing ourselves as adults? How many times do we say what would seem right but never exactly how we feel? How many times do we have to look like we are keeping it together but falling apart on the inside?

I would hold back on telling people how I feel about them just because I didn't want to sound sappy. One thing God revealed about me is that I am a very loving and affectionate person. I laughed at that because even though I can be affectionate to others, I hold back on it with certain people if I feel like they won't respond to it in the manner I desire. But I'm learning you have to let people respond in a way that is suitable for them.

So, as much as I wanted to deny parts of myself just because I couldn't fully identify with them, God wanted to show me piece by piece. I heard the words, you're musically inclined, very artistic, very creative, silly, goofy, playful, outgoing with certain people and very strategic. So, the first word that came to my mind was where. I don't see this very creative woman or this very artistic woman that you are speaking to me about. I surely don't see this musically inclined woman you are speaking of.

I had to choose to stop looking at what I saw in myself in those moments. I had to allow God to show me these characteristics in myself over time while also referring back to who I was as a little girl. The one jumping and laughing around the house was still in me. The little girl tapping/making drum beats on the furniture was musically inclined and the little girl recreating pictures was very artistic. So, I had to ask myself that very important question again. Am I willing to follow what God says about me regardless of what I look like to everyone else?

LESSON 5 SELF-LOVE/ACCEPTANCE

How can you love on others if you don't fully love on yourself? The hardest thing I wanted to do was love on everyone else but not love on myself. I did it for years not realizing that it was detrimental to myself.

How can you wake up every morning and look in the mirror but not really like anything about yourself? It was so easy for me to praise everyone else's accomplishments and value what everyone else had to offer the world, but I couldn't do the same when it came to myself. I didn't feel like I had anything to offer the world. I was so hard on myself whenever I made a mistake but was quick to reassure anyone else who did the same thing. I couldn't show myself compassion but was willing to give it to everyone else.

Even when it came to my relationship with God, I would get mad at myself when I would mess up or when I strayed from doing something in the way I thought I should. I thought I should have my bible read by this certain time, I should know this amount of scriptures and pray for these amounts of topics. But really, I was giving myself a burden that God never placed on me. I was making it seem like God would only truly love me if I could accomplish all these things for Him. I didn't have any real love and compassion for myself, so I had a hard time accepting God's.

I had a hard time accepting God's love for me outside of what I could get done in a day or how well I did something. I had a hard time accepting love for myself outside of what I could do for others; outside of how much they acknowledged and praised it. I desired for people to love the gifts and the things I did for them because in return it gave me that acceptance to love myself.

I like to care deeply for others. But I wasn't doing it in a healthy way. I would feel upset if I felt like people weren't responding to my help in a loving manner, or they didn't respond at all. The other direction I would go down was attaching my self-esteem to it. I thought well of myself if people enjoyed what I could do for them and I thought less of myself if they didn't. Either way, none of these routes were healthy and they showed me how little I loved/thought of myself.

Sometimes when we don't love ourselves, we can close off love all together. We may not allow other people to love us because we don't fully love us. Maybe there were people in our life that weren't able to love us in the way we needed. Maybe there were people we hung around that didn't love us in the way that they should have. Or maybe we just didn't fully get an opportunity to show love in the way we desired to. Why would she want to love me like that? My own mother didn't love me like that. Why would she want to be friends with me? I don't trust other women like that.

For others, we end up clinging to love so badly that we allow anything and everything to happen to us. We stay in relationships and friendships that should have definitely ended a while ago. Wanting to be loved so badly can be dangerous to our mental, spiritual, emotional and sometimes our physical health.

But the truth is, we all want someone to love us, our flaws and all. We all want someone who will see past the walls that we build up and know that we desire love. For me, it started with God. I had to understand that he wasn't going to hurt me in the way that my parents did and that He is a perfect father. He would forgive my mistakes and still love on me when I went astray. He would wait on me to come back. I didn't have to hold every failure and mistake over my head. To be honest, some of the things I saw as failure was just lessons to Him. But I couldn't fully learn to love myself until I saw that God didn't see me as stupid, dumb or anything else outside of what He says about me.

I don't have to earn any kind of love. I could give myself grace because He gives me grace. I am favored because He favors me. I am loved regardless. God's love for me helped me manage how I loved on myself and how I loved on others. I was no longer interested in being in relationships with men who couldn't love and protect me in the way that God does. I was no longer interested in friendships that weren't growing and adding any value to my life. I was no longer interested in things that I wasn't willing to pray over.

One night, I was complaining about how tired I was of living this life and I heard "Are you willing to pray over the life that you want?" I had to sit back and think of why I stopped praying over the things I desired. I was living life like I assumed they would come one day in just the manner that they should. But if I really wanted to love my life, I had to be willing to pray over the things I wanted to love.

LESSON 6 WHERE'S YOUR VOICE?

There are some people in my life who I've had the most estranged relationships with from time to time. You may be able to guess that it's my family members. There are times when I love to be around them and then other times, they honestly irk my nerves. But what family doesn't? One thing I hated as a teenager was being told you should get to know your other family members. I guess I hated this so much because to me it signified that you want me to get to know other people when you barely know me.

So, getting to know other family members: I'm not saying I'm perfect, but I really don't enjoy getting together to have superficial conversations while talking about everyone's business. It's no fun sitting around a bunch of people and acting like we are the perfect family with no problems while trying to hear everyone else's problems. It's no fun being the keep up with the Joneses family. None of those things were attractive to me growing up but I never was going to voice that out loud.

So, why did I feel like I had an estranged relationship with my family members? Well, there are a number of different reasons that we might be able to name toward why we no longer feel as close to certain people. As I began to go on this journey of discovering myself, I had to come to terms with unpleasant memories from certain family members that were holding me back. One particular family member was my grandfather. I remember one night when I was younger, I was arguing with my family about not having to clean a room that I didn't make the mess in. It got heated to a point where my grandfather had me leaning over the kitchen sink holding me by my neck because I didn't want to clean the room.

Another family member that I felt I had an estranged relationship with was my mother. I mean we never fully had the best relationship after my great grandmother passed away. But I couldn't understand why we would have meaningful conversations only for me to be mad again in a few days. There were times when my mom just wasn't willing to hear my voice because she wanted to say what she thought was right. She would talk over you and drown out your voice like your opinion didn't matter.

I've also had other family members who drowned out my voice because they wanted to speak what they thought was right. I felt so unheard and it was pretty hurtful to be done by different people in my life. Sometimes you learn to live with your voice not being heard. She's just quiet. What does she have to say? She's so young. What does she know? He doesn't have a degree. Are you sure he knows what he's talking about?

But that's not the way I want to live my life anymore. I don't want to live a life where people are able to shut me down through intimidation. I don't want to live a life where I feel like we all need to shrink back because this person can't handle the truth, or we don't want to rock the boat. At the end of the day, I need to be able to stay true to myself whether you like me or not. I don't have to be rude and nasty to get my point across, but I actually do need to be able to open my mouth.

LESSON 7 NEW PEOPLE

I studied a little bit about Joseph (Genesis chapter 37 **Joseph Dreams Of Greatness**, NKJV) while writing this portion. I noticed how Joseph had dreams about his life that no one else could really understand. He was eager to tell his family members of his dreams, but they couldn't really see them the way he did. "Please hear this dream which I have dreamed: There we were, binding sheaves in the field. Then behold, my sheaf arose and also stood upright; and indeed your sheaves stood all around and bowed down to my sheaf (Genesis 37:6-7).

Joseph's brothers responded to his dream. And his brothers said to him, "Shall you indeed reign over us? Or shall you indeed have dominion over us?" (Genesis 37:8). He also told his family about his second dream.

So he told it to his father and his brothers; and his father rebuked him and said to him, "What is this dream that you have dreamed? Shall your mother and I and your brothers indeed come to bow down to the earth before you?" (Genesis 37:10).

Joseph's story has a lot more context pertaining to the jealousy of his brothers toward his dreams. But I want to focus on the pieces I really got from the story. His story has taught me that sometimes the people around you won't be able to see what dreams and goals you are aiming for. Those dreams and goals may not even make sense to anyone around you. At the same time, you may have to surround yourself with people who can help you see your dreams more clearly. The people in your current environment (even with the best of their abilities) may not have what you need or know what you need. But the right people will. I say **right** because not just any person is meant for your life.

There came a point where I didn't fully know what I needed but I knew it was more than what I had. I was willing to move forward and let it unfold before my eyes.

LESSON 8 THE REALIGNMENT

Being in alignment with who I've always been isn't the easiest thing to do. I'm reminded of the pieces of me that I struggled to identify with, but I also surrender to the new and improved pieces of me. I have to surrender to the need for me to connect to others in a deeper manner. I have to surrender to feeling my own emotions rather than dissociating from them.

I learned to put everyone else's emotions before my own. I allowed family members to tell me what was best for me and my life. In return, I suppressed what I thought about myself and what I saw fit for my life. I suppressed my concerns and my questioning of things. The crazy thing is I always tried to make myself believe and feel like what everyone else wanted to be true. I tried to force myself to not feel the emotions I was feeling, the sadness I felt, the anger, the resentment and the tiredness. I knew I had people around me who would tell me reasons why I shouldn't feel the way

I felt. So, rather than dealing with my true emotions, I was forcing other emotions on myself for years.

I felt bad for not really feeling the way everyone else wanted me to feel. I felt like I had to hide how unhappy I was with myself and with my life. But really hiding my unhappiness was causing more damage than good. Talk about being out of alignment with who you are. I had to really own up to how unhappy I was. I had to get around people who were willing to let me release it; who didn't expect me to keep playing happy. I needed people who didn't silently judge me, who didn't talk about me when I left the room, and who didn't already have a comment waiting for me on why I'm not trying enough.

It takes courage to really admit that you aren't happy with yourself or with your life. Many people walk around faking happiness and hiding from their real situations. Many people feel guilty for being unhappy because there may be someone out there worse off. Usually there are people worse off than us. But I hated when those words were used just so I could settle for what I had. I believe there is usually something we can do to make our life a little bit more fulfilling. For me, I had to reconnect with God and my true self to see that.

WHAT'S NEXT?

I hope my story has or will cause you to look at your story and situation. We all have stories that are unique to us. But I also believe we may find similarities to the stories of others if we look deep enough. So, where do you go from here?

I hope you look deep enough into your story and draw out pieces that may need to have some work done. We all have a journey that is meant for us and it's up to us to move toward it. Maybe you need to no longer allow life to determine your joy. Maybe you need to make peace with what you've experienced and choose to live a better life. In the process, I hope you experience joy and pleasures along your way. I hope you come in contact with those who will add to your peace and joy.

I pray you give yourself grace and encouragement as you walk in your path. There are times where we look at our life and think we should be at a certain point by now. Sometimes we allow other people's desires for us to make us feel like we should be at a certain point. In reality, none of us are perfect. We all make mistakes and we might even have setbacks. So, we have to allow our journey to be our journey and no one else's. We have to allow our healing to be the healing that is meant for us. We have to allow the timing to be the timing that is meant for us. Find those areas in your life that you know would be better off by surrendering to God. Choose to live a life that is meant for you in the best way possible.

I would love to stay in touch. Follow me on Instagram at @inspiringdaze and please leave a book review. I want to know where your journey will lead you.

CPSIA information can be obtained
at www.ICGtesting.com
Printed in the USA
BVHW031647040221
599249BV00002B/336